A FRIENDLY GUIDE TO JESUS

ANDREW HAMILTON SJ

Published by
John Garratt Publishing
32 Glenvale Crescent
Mulgrave, Vic. 3170
www.johngarratt.com.au

Copyright ©2010 Andrew Hamilton SJ

All rights reserved. Except as provided by the Australian copyright law, no part of this book may be reproduced in any way without permission in writing from the publisher.

Design and typesetting by Lynne Muir
Text editing by Ann M Philpott

All images are ©Jan Hynes – used with permission.

Cataloguing-in-Publication information for this title is available from the National Library of Australia.
www.nla.gov.au

ISBN 9781920721978

Nihil Obstat : Reverend Gerard Diamond MA (Oxon), LSS, D Theol Diocesan Censor
Imprimatur : Most Reverend Les Tomlinson DD Titular Bishop of Siniti, Vicar General
Date : 16th September 2010
The Nihil Obstat and Imprimatur are official declarations that a book or pamphlet is free of doctrinal or moral error. No implication is contained therein that those who have granted the Nihil Obstat and Imprimatur agree with the contents, opinions or statements expressed. They do not necessarily signify that the work is approved as a basic text for catechetical instruction.

Scripture quotations are drawn from the *New Revised Standard Version of the Bible*, copyright ©1989 by the Division of Christian Education of the National Council of the Churches of Christ in the USA. Used by permission. All rights reserved.

Throughout this book Jan Hynes's stunning paintings of the urban landscape of contemporary Australia, as well as one of Australian wilderness, illustrate the life of Jesus in a fresh and vivid way. Her explanations of the imagery in each painting add layers of meaning to the viewer's experience. The settings for Jan's paintings are in and around her home town, Townsville, a regional city in Northern Australia.

Contents

Prologue   5

Preface: The big questions   7

1: Jesus as a Jewish young man   9

    The God of Israel

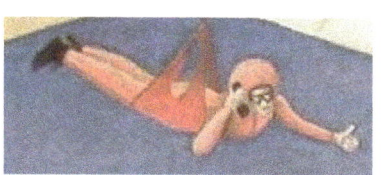
2: Jesus in the gospels   13

    Christians' responses to the gospel stories

3: Stories of Jesus' birth   19

    The infancy gospels

4: Jesus with people   23

    Jesus' public life

5: The invitation to follow Jesus   27

    Jesus and discipleship

6: Jesus' death   31

    Finding meaning in Jesus' death

7: Jesus' rising from the dead   35

    Finding meaning in Jesus' rising

8: The Son of God   39

    Jesus as the Son of God

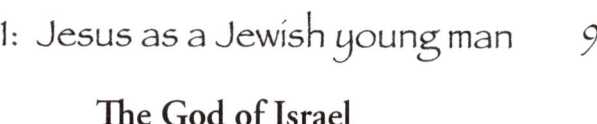
9: Jesus and the Church   43

    Finding Jesus

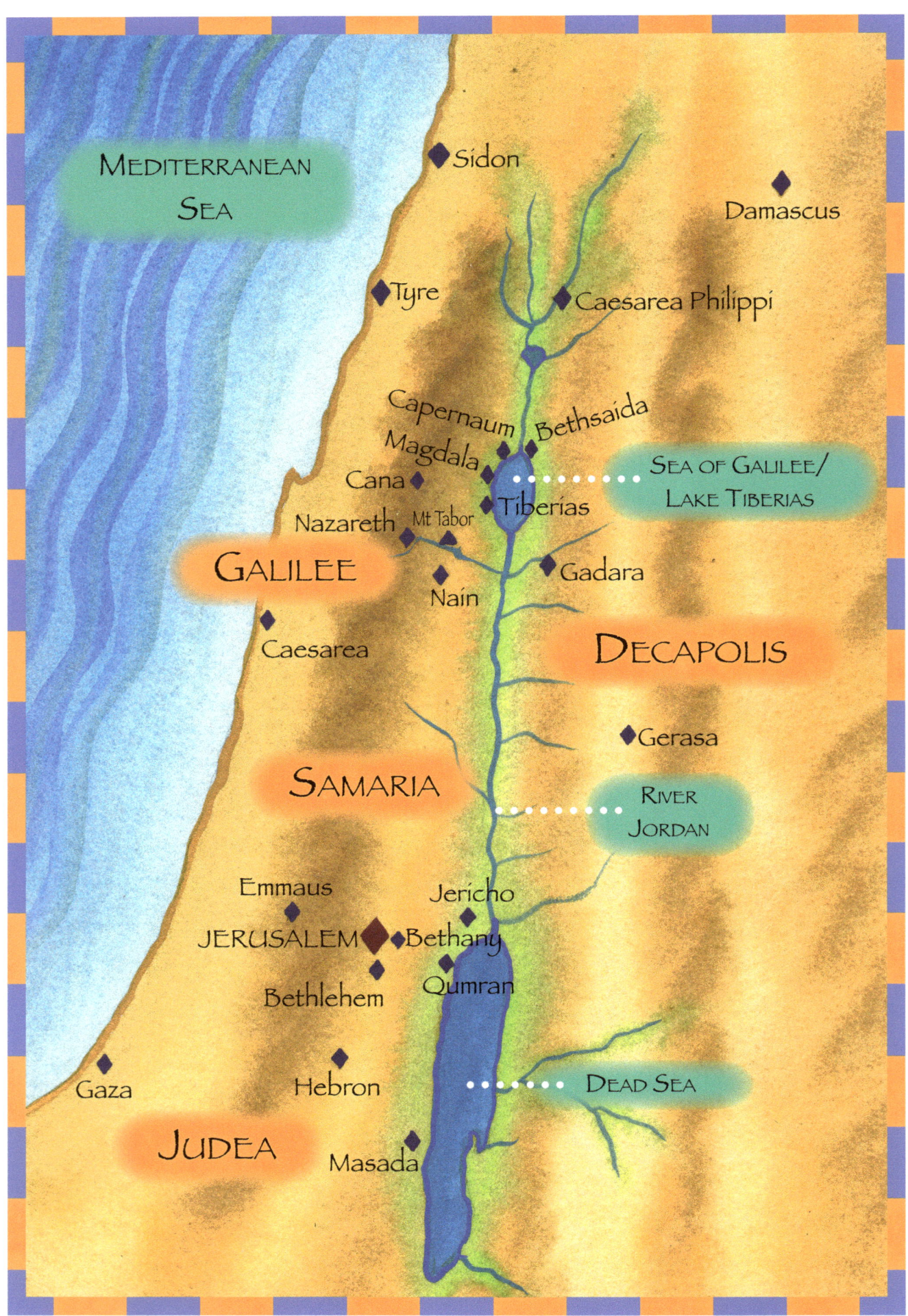

Prologue

Recently I was talking with a group of senior students from Catholic schools. They were lively and interesting. I asked them how they found their religion classes. Some complained that they were a distraction from the real business of passing their VCE. But generally they were surprisingly positive. 'Religion classes give us a chance to talk about big questions,' one said.

Then another added, 'The trouble is, just when we get interested, the teacher insists on talking about Jesus.' There were groans and general agreement. So I asked them why Jesus was such a turn-off. One said that it was like when 'hot gospellers' come to the front door. 'They start by asking you if you are concerned about the environment or the recession. If you say you are, they say, "Well, the answer is in the Bible." And then they go on and on about the Bible. They pretend to be interested in big issues, but what they're really interested in is their religion.'

I was reminded of the story of the big sign erected outside a church. It announced, 'Jesus is the answer.' Underneath it someone had written in big letters, 'Yeah, but what is the question?'

Young people are right to be asking big questions. They want to explore what their lives and the world are about.

But they don't just want big answers to these questions. They want answers that will make a difference in their lives. They want to know how to live happily and well. So do we all.

That is what faith in Jesus is about.

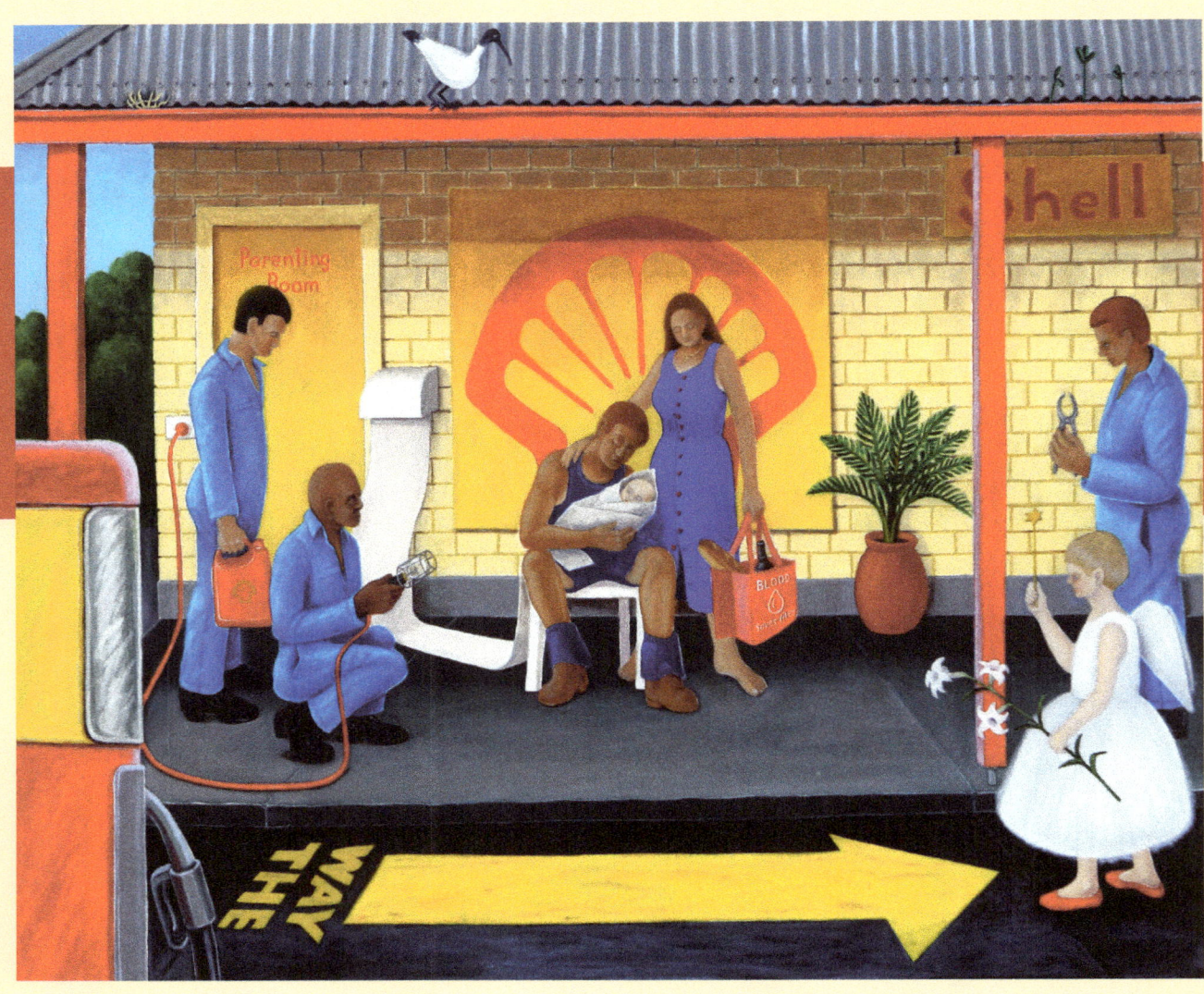

Bonding time: the nativity in Townsville

The location of this picture is a service station, as stables are no longer found in our urban environment. Garage workers replace the shepherds as they tend the newly born baby Jesus. One carries a light (the light that Jesus is to bring to the world); the second carries a tool of his trade, hinting at the instruments of the birthing process; and the third mechanic carries oil (a reference to the handmaiden oil lamps, the good oil spiritual grace, illumination and benediction, the anointing of kings and the perfumed oils mentioned in the New Testament on several occasions). Oil is a symbol in many cultures of consecration, dedication and wisdom.

The golden Shell logo, symbolic of birth (Botticelli's *Birth of Venus*, 1482) is commonly used in religious paintings. In many cultures it is linked with conception, regeneration and baptism. It is also a reference to Christian pilgrimage (St Christopher's attribute).

Joseph, being a modern father, was present at the birth and holds the baby Jesus, demonstrating the connection of bonding. As there are no swaddling clothes, Jesus is wrapped in lengths of paper towelling, the only thing available at the service station in the parenting room. Some see the paper towelling as a reference to the ancestry of the Old Testament going back to the tribes of Israel. Joseph wears his carpenter's clothes.

Mary wears her blue dress, the colour used to suggest spirituality. The dress opens from the front to facilitate breastfeeding her baby. The buttons are red (for blood) and heart-shaped (indicating her love for her baby). Mary carries a red shopping bag bearing the Red Cross slogan of 'Blood saves lives', portending Jesus' death on the cross to save the lives of believers. In the bag a stick of bread and a bottle of red wine represent the sacrament of Communion.

The potted palm equates to the Tree of Life (Egypt and Arabia) and the New Testament reference to Palm Sunday. It is also a reference to the Virgin Mary – 'you are stately as a palm tree' (Song of Solomon 7:7).

The yellow 'The Way' sign on the driveway shows the way to salvation. The arrow points to a young girl dressed in a fairy outfit but evoking an angel as she holds a lily (Christmas/Easter lily) and a gold star (Star of Bethlehem).

On the roof is an ibis (the Holy Spirit) and three sprouting seedlings (the Trinity and the three crosses of Calvary).

Preface: The big questions

There is not much point thinking about Jesus unless he helps us see what matters. The worst thing we can do to Jesus is to tame him and to see him as interested only in small questions that are not central in our lives.

What matters is summed up in questions like these: Why are we here in the world? What are we to make of our world, so beautiful and so spoiled, with so much beauty and so much suffering? What will become of us as individuals and as a species? How should we live in the world and with other people? Are we really loveable, and are we capable of loving other people? Why do some of us enjoy such good fortune while others suffer so much?

When we ask these questions, we are not just looking for correct answers. We also want to know how we should live in our world. Christians look for answers to these questions in the story of Jesus. We believe that we shall see our world more clearly and live in it more richly when we follow Jesus.

Jesus does not answer our big questions by giving us information or telling us how our world works. When we follow him he takes us to a place from which we can ask questions helpfully. It is like the old Irish joke in which a traveller asks a local how he can get to Limerick. The local answers, 'If I were going to Limerick, I wouldn't start from here.' The answer isn't very helpful for the traveller. But it is amusing because we instinctively recognise its truth.

There are some questions we can ask, but we won't get any helpful answers until we are in the right place. For example, if I am greedy and self-centred, and ask 'what is in it for me' when asked to visit elderly relatives in hospital, no one will be able to give me a satisfactory answer. I am in the wrong place. I would need to be open to the subtle ways in which people can bless me when I act unselfishly towards them.

> The next day John again was standing with two of his disciples, and as he watched Jesus walk by, he exclaimed, 'Look, here is the Lamb of God!' The two disciples heard him say this, and they followed Jesus. When Jesus turned and saw them following, he said to them, 'What are you looking for?' They said to him, 'Rabbi' (which translated means Teacher), 'where are you staying?' He said to them, 'Come and see.' They came and saw where he was staying, and they remained with him that day. It was about four o'clock in the afternoon.
>
> John 1: 35–39

Christian faith invites us to follow Jesus in order to discover what really matters in our lives and to show us how we can live well. Jesus' path begins with a God who loves each of us enough to create a world for us and to care for us from birth to death. This love led God's Son to become poor for us and to join us in the messiness of our lives. It inspired him to love us enough to endure great hostility and to give his life for us. It concluded with his rising to new life and his helping us live in a new relationship with God and one another.

By following Jesus on that path we can see that God really matters, that God's love for us really matters, and that accepting God's love and being open to the love of others really matters. Because these things matter we are encouraged to respond by a simple and generous way of life.

In the wilderness

The setting is Mt Stuart, a mountain not far from Townsville in Northern Australia where aerials for telecommunications can be seen (to receive and transmit messages). These aerials also represent the three crosses on the hill of Calvary. The landscape depicts the scene after a bushfire when the ground is bare and the surface rock is exposed. The country is in drought and under such conditions it appears as a real wilderness with rocky ground.

Termite mounds are common in many parts of northern Australia and are generally viewed as signs of devastation (although the termites do perform a useful role in the ecology of a region).

The lizard or monitor is a large reptile, feared by most as unpleasant. It functions as a substitute for the snake as a symbol of temptation in the wilderness. There are echoes of the Garden of Eden.

There are a number of other objects of interest in this picture. The crow – the bird and its black colour – is a symbol of death in the mythology of many cultures. The telegraph pole represents the cross, especially with the crow sitting on it. The bush has been burnt (reminiscent of the flaming bush). The twelve branches represent the twelve tribes of Israel. There is a chasm, which hints at the chasm of the future. Storm clouds on the horizon indicate a stormy time ahead for Jesus once he comes out of the wilderness.

1: Jesus as a Jewish young man

One of the joys of my life as a priest has been to serve a small Cambodian Catholic community as their chaplain. They came as refugees to Australia. I had met many of them in the Thai camps where they lived after fleeing from Pol Pot's terrible regime.

At first we had trouble understanding one another, particularly when it came to making arrangements. They ticked me off for saying no to invitations I could not accept. And I was frustrated when I asked people if they would like to gather for Mass or for a picnic, and they would say yes, but then no one turned up. They thought that I was a bit rude; I thought they were rude.

Only gradually did I realise that what I thought to be rudeness was really sensitivity. In Cambodian culture, which was shaped by Buddhism, what matters is to live well and to make other people happy. This meant that we should answer questions in a way that makes the questioner happy. If people asked me if I could go to a wedding, they would be happy if I said yes. So I should have said yes in a neutral way, and then not have gone. When I invited the Cambodians to Mass or to a picnic, they could see that I would be delighted if they said yes. So they said yes. But in their own culture, yes often means no. They knew the difference between a real yes and a polite yes. I still had to learn the difference.

When we try to say what matters to us, we always do so within our own culture. Birthday parties say that our family and friends matter to us. Marriage celebrations say how much it matters to us to be faithful in our love. We show our respect for those who have died in battle in Anzac Day services. We don't need to find words for what matters. Parties, weddings and remembrances say it all for us. When we meet people from other cultures, we need to explore the ways in which they express what matters to them.

If we want to follow Jesus and learn what matters and how we can live happily, we need to understand something of his culture. He was born in Palestine. Like his fellow Jews, he found the meaning of his life and of his world in the story of the God of Israel who had made the world and whose love was shown in the history of Israel.

Jesus' relationship to the God of Israel was expressed through prayer, time spent at the temple, reflection on God's words in the Jewish scriptures, and in all the ritual that went with Jewish daily life.

The God of Israel

Jewish people of Jesus' time found the answer to their large questions in the story of their God. They saw God as the Lord of the whole world, but particularly as the God of Israel. God had chosen Israel to be his people, and they found their meaning in being part of God's chosen people.

Being chosen as God's people meant that they were loved dearly by God and were under God's protection. It also meant that they were to respond to God's choice by living generously. The Jews understood their own history as lived between these two poles of being dearly loved and of responding, often badly, to God's love. Their history was like a long domestic dispute in which they were unfaithful, were thrown out of home, welcomed back and forgiven, and were again unfaithful. They saw the meaning of their lives in terms of sin and being forgiven and always loved.

They also dwelt on the key moments of their history. They saw these as their release from slavery in Egypt to become an independent nation, and their exile in Babylon when the temple was destroyed and the people apparently scattered forever. God was at work in their formation as a people and in their scattering and return. God was also present in the Israel of Jesus' day, when the people did it hard under Roman rule.

Their history taught the Jewish people to hope that God would again intervene in their national life. They looked forward to the day when God would free Israel and would himself rule the world. For many Jews, this hope was associated with the belief that God would one day raise to life the faithful who had died.

At the centre of Jewish life were the temple and the Law that was given to Moses. In these they found a way of living that would be happy and would please God. In the temple they could celebrate the great events of Israel's history through which God had worked, and make sacrifices for their sins. It was the great sign that God was present among the people God had chosen.

The scriptures often spoke of the Spirit of God. The Spirit was associated with God's action in the world, and was also given to people through whom God worked. In Jesus' time people waited for the coming of God among his people. Then the Spirit would be with the people, giving them life and intimacy with God. The Spirit would give them victory over all the things that made for death.

These were the large things of Jewish life. But they were also attentive to God on a day-to-day basis. They found space to reflect in the synagogue where they heard the scriptures explained and applied to their own daily life. Many, especially the Pharisees, found a way of responding generously to God's love through living by the laws governing everyday life. These laws embraced eating, washing, fasting, how to spend the Sabbath day of rest, and who to invite to meals. Through their obedience to the Law they could make God matter in every detail of their lives.

This was the world that Jesus entered. These were the ways in which he was taught what mattered, and how this was related to the history of God's relationship with the people of Israel.

> **The meaning of the Law**
> When your children ask you in time to come, 'What is the meaning of the decrees and the statutes and the ordinances that the Lord our God has commanded you?' then you shall say to your children, 'We were Pharaoh's slaves in Egypt, but the Lord brought us out of Egypt with a mighty hand. The Lord displayed before our eyes great and awesome signs and wonders against Egypt, against Pharaoh and all his household. He brought us out from there in order to bring us in, to give us the land that he promised on oath to our ancestors.
>
> Deuteronomy 6.20–23

The Old Testament

The Old Testament is not a history book. It is less interested in dates than in the stages of God's relationship to Israel. Here are some of the significant writings and the way they describe God's relationship to the people of Israel.

The Beginnings

The stories of the book of Genesis describe our dependence on God, the way sin works in our world, and God's constancy in a love that outweighs sin. The stories also speak of the beginnings and the surprising twists and turns of God's special choice of Israel.

Liberation from Egypt

The core of the faith of Israel was the memory of how God freed them from Egypt where they were slaves, led them into their land and gave them a way of life that depended on God. This story is told in spectacular ways by the Books of Exodus, Deuteronomy, Leviticus and Judges. At the heart of the story is a God who stays with the people even when they abandon him.

The Kingdom of Israel

One of the crucial decisions made by Israel was to have a king to rule them. The Books of Samuel, of Kings and of Chronicles describe the growth of Israel under David and his successors, and its later division and catastrophic defeat by the Assyrians. The people of Jerusalem were exiled to Babylon, and their faith in their God seemed discredited. Later they returned to Jerusalem, rebuilt their temple and again found God in their history.

The Biblical writers reflected on where God was in the Exile and in their return to Jerusalem. They emphasised Israel's consistent unfaithfulness and God's unfailing refusal to give up on his people.

The Prophets

When reflecting on the meaning of the Exile and on how they could live faithfully, people found great help in the writings of the prophets. The prophets spoke for God when judging the public events of their day. The prophets promised that God would lead Israel to a better time and a better world, which kept hope alive in a dark time when God seemed to have abandoned them. The prophets kept speaking about what really mattered, and how people should live.

The Writings

Many books in the Old Testament cannot easily be classified. They are often called simply the Writings. They helped Israel to reflect on where God is to be found. They include stories like that of Tobias, romances, prayers for public worship and personal use (the Psalms), discussions of challenging religious questions (Job) and reflections on how to live faithfully. They all invite their readers to recognise that God never gives up on the people he has chosen, and remind them that ultimately it is God who matters.

Entering the city: Palm Sunday

The picture shows the mall in the city centre with the surrounding buildings. Castle Hill looms over the city, portending the hill of Calvary. The red carpet is rolled out to welcome Jesus as it would be for an important official guest. The crowd forms an arch of palm branches as might be made for a guard of honour at a football grand final or for a bridal couple on exiting a church after their marriage ceremony. A jogger arrives late to join the crowd.

The clock indicates that it is a few minutes to twelve. Metaphorically, there is not much time left. Jesus chooses to enter the city by bicycle. Asses are not an option in twenty-first century Townsville, and public transport is virtually non-existent. His choice of bicycle is egalitarian and sound ecologically. His red bicycle helmet alludes to the blood of the crown of thorns. His white T-shirt is for purity and the blue shorts are for spirituality. But these are just ordinary clothes – no fancy lycra cycling gear.

There is a man 'sitting on the fence', unable to decide what his choice will be. Several street signs allude to Jesus' dilemma. A red sign (blood) reads 'CROSSing AHEAD' and warns of the imminent death on the cross. A traffic light shows green to cross the street, but also says 'WAIT'. On the other side of the street, a parking sign reads 'NO STANDING', portending that once the decision has been made there is no stopping or going back.

Where is the Holy Spirit? It could be in the dark storm clouds gathering in the background. It could be in the young child in the stroller. It is the viewer's choice.

2: Jesus in the gospels

When people reflect together on gospel stories about Jesus, they usually find deep and personal meanings in them. These meanings are often astonishingly different.

I once heard two women give very different interpretations of the story of Martha and Mary in Luke's Gospel. You might remember the story: Martha and younger sister Mary are entertaining Jesus in Martha's house. Mary is sitting at Jesus' feet listening to him while Martha is busily preparing the food. In exasperation Martha asks Jesus to tell Mary to give her a hand. Jesus turns on Martha and says that what Mary is doing is more important.

The first of the women to comment on this story was born in Australia. She had a grown-up family. She imagined Martha as rushing around and getting frustrated. So she became annoyed with Mary who just wanted to listen quietly to Jesus. She saw something of both Martha and Mary in herself. She liked Jesus' remark because it encouraged her to free herself from the temptation to be driven and compulsively busy. For her the story was about encouraging inner freedom and finding the space she needed to nourish it.

The second woman to comment on the story was younger and unmarried. She had recently come to Australia from India. For her, the key to the story was that Martha owned the house. In her culture it was expected that, in return for board and lodging, the younger sister would do all the housework. So Martha did not complain to Jesus simply because she was busy. She simply asked him to remind Mary of her duty as a younger sister and boarder.

In her reading it was significant that Mary was sitting at Jesus' feet. This was the place where teachers' disciples always sit as they prepare themselves to go out and teach. So Mary was not just listening. She was preparing to be an active disciple of Jesus. When Jesus answered Martha, he was telling her that Mary's commitment to be a disciple was more important than her conventional duties in the home. The young Indian woman found the story encouraging because it told her that she was free to find new ways of following Jesus in her new culture. She did not have to remain trapped by the expectations of her own culture.

Both these women found that the story of Martha and Mary helped them to discover what really mattered in their lives. For both women, too, the story pointed to how they should live. But each of them drew distinctively different lessons from the story that corresponded to their situation and their culture.

Most of us learn about Jesus through the stories of the gospels. They throw light on our lives too. But how do the gospels help us to follow Jesus, and how can it be right for people to read the gospel stories about Jesus in such different ways?

Christians' responses to the gospel stories

At the heart of the gospels is the large story about Jesus' death and resurrection. For the early hearers of the gospels Jesus' crucifixion and rising from the dead were central events. They told them that following Jesus was the way to understand what really matters in life and how to live happily.

The early Christians shared Jesus' Jewish background. So they found what mattered in the story of God's relationship with the people of Israel. They found God's love shown in the making of the world and in calling the people out of slavery in Egypt to be God's people. They found a way of living that responded to God's love in the feasts and sacrifices celebrated in the temple, and also in faithfully living their daily lives following the scriptural instructions about eating, fasting, washing and so on, and nurturing the hope that God would again intervene decisively in the history of their people.

In Jesus' death and resurrection they found a surprising and radical vision of God's love. If they were tempted to say that God loved and chose only the good and faithful Jewish people who did God's will, Jesus' death and resurrection blew their minds. Here was a God whose intervention came in the life of a man who was not a victorious commander. He was tortured and killed as a criminal would have been killed at that time. His story was not one of being faithful to the Law, but of being cursed by the Law through the way he died. He was made a nothing, and in Jesus God showed that he loved dearly people who were sinners and nothings. God's love could not be restricted to any one nation or to the decent and faithful people among that nation. In his rising from the dead, Jesus showed that God's love had changed their world and that there was a new way to live – by loving even their enemies.

That was the message the first Christians brought others. They spoke of a God who had shown himself and acted decisively through the death and the resurrection of Jesus. They illustrated this first gospel with stories and sayings of Jesus.

Later on these stories and sayings were brought together into the larger collection of stories that we know as the Gospel, meaning the 'Good News'. In the gospels, especially Mark's Gospel, which was probably the first to be written, the story of Jesus' death is recounted at length. It receives so much space because it is the heart of the gospel message. The gospels were not written first of all to give us details about the life of Jesus, but to teach Christians that the answer to all the deep questions about human life and the world was to be found in following Jesus.

Presumably the first gospel proved to be such a successful form of teaching that other gospel writers used it to address the deep questions their communities were asking about their lives, but in a way that spoke directly to the different issues each community was experiencing. Luke and Matthew therefore relate the stories told by Mark in slightly different ways in order to make points for their own audiences.

That is why two readers of the story of Martha and Mary can interpret it in such different ways. Just as the Holy Spirit made Christ vividly alive to the different communities addressed by the gospel writers, so the Spirit today enables different readers to understand Jesus in fresh ways. To follow Jesus takes each of us along our own path, but we share a common faith that makes us look to Jesus to show us what matters and where our path will lead.

For later readers of the gospels, like ourselves, the gospels are important because they allow us to imagine Jesus. He is not simply the Son of God who died and rose for us, but a figure of flesh and blood who acts decisively, is deep and passionate in his relationships, is a wonderful and observant storyteller, and gives himself fully to his mission. When we imagine Jesus, we can also imagine what God is like. Jesus embodies in the stories of the gospels the compassion, interest and attitudes of God. As we look at him, we find a way of addressing the deep questions we ask ourselves.

> Now as they went on their way, he entered a certain village, where a woman named Martha welcomed him into her home. She had a sister named Mary, who sat at the Lord's feet and listened to what he was saying. But Martha was distracted by her many tasks; so she came to him and asked, 'Lord, do you not care that my sister has left me to do all the work by myself? Tell her then to help me.' But the Lord answered her, 'Martha, Martha, you are worried and distracted by many things; there is need of only one thing. Mary has chosen the better part, which will not be taken away from her.'
>
> Luke 10:38–42

Telling the story of Jesus

The early Christians had to find ways to help people believe in Christ and to grow in their faith. At first they did this by summarising the core of their faith, which they illustrated by the stories and sayings of Jesus. In his letters to the churches he had founded, the earliest writings of the New Testament, St Paul expanded on this basic teaching, applying it to the new situations he met. He always referred to Jesus Christ, and particularly to his death and resurrection.

The gospel writers gathered together the stories and sayings of Jesus and shaped them into an overarching story. They helped answer people's questions about Jesus, focusing on Jesus' significance in God's plan.

Mark's Gospel

Mark's Gospel was probably the first gospel to have been written. Mark may have written it in a time of persecution. His work is short and confronting, consisting of tersely told stories, undecorated sayings of Jesus and sharp images. Mark focuses on Jesus' path to death in Jerusalem and on his disciples' call to follow him. His work is consoling because he shows that even though the faith of Jesus' disciples was weak and unsteady in their commitment, Jesus never stopped working with them.

Matthew's Gospel

Matthew and Luke may both have adapted Mark's Gospel to their own purposes, but they also drew on other collections of Jesus' sayings. Mathew wrote especially for an audience with a Jewish background. His gospel reflects a conflict between the Jewish Christians and the Jews with whom they had parted company when they became Christian. The Jesus of Matthew's Gospel acts like a Jewish religious teacher. Matthew shows that faith in Christ not only fulfils the promises of the Jewish scriptures, but also goes beyond them.

Luke's Gospel

The Gospel of Luke is part of a two-volume work. It was followed by the Acts of the Apostles, which describes the spread of the Church after Jesus' resurrection. The Holy Spirit is central in Luke's Gospel. Jesus is conceived by the power of the Spirit, led by the Spirit, preaches the coming of the Spirit, and gives the Spirit to the Church through his resurrection. Jesus' life bears the mark of the Spirit. He is a model for all Christians in their lives.

The fourth gospel

The fourth gospel, attributed to John, differs markedly from the other gospels. It has its own stories of Jesus, and gives many long speeches to him. It presents Jesus in a majestic and mysterious way. He is fully in control of every situation. When we look at Jesus we see God at work. But this gospel also describes Jesus' humanity. He weeps for his friend, and is tired after walking in the heat of the day. The message of John's Gospel is that God can be found in the human life of Jesus.

Parables of Jesus

Story	Matthew	Mark	Luke
Growing seed		4:26-29	
Two debtors			7:41-43
Salt without taste	5:13	9:50	14:34-35
Lamp under a bushel	5:14-15	4:21-23	8:16-18
Good Samaritan			10:30-37
Friend at night			11:5-8
Rich fool			12:16-21
Wise and foolish builders	7:24-27		6:46-49
New cloth on an old garment	9:16	2:21	5:36
New wine into old wineskins	9:17	2:22	5:37-39
Strong man	12:29	3:27	11:21-22
Sower	13:3-9, 18-21	4:3-9, 14-20	8:5-8, 11-15
Tares	13:24-30		
Barren fig tree			13:6-9
Mustard seed	13:31-32	4:30-32	13:18-19
Leaven	13:33		13:20-21
Hidden treasure	13:44		
Pearl of great value	13:45		
Drawing in the net	13:47-50		
Counting the cost			14:28-33
Lost sheep	18:10-14		15:4-7
Unforgiving servant	18:23-35		
Lost coin			15:8-10
Prodigal son			15:11-32
Unjust steward			16:1-13
Rich man and Lazarus			16:19-31
Master and servant			17:7-10
Unjust judge and persistent widow			18:1-8
Pharisee and the tax collector			18:9-14
Workers in the vineyard	20:1-6		
Two sons	21:28-32		
Wicked tenants	21:33-41	12:1-9	20:9-16
Wedding feast	22:1-14		
Places of honour at the feast			14:7-14
Great banquet and reluctant guests			14:16-24
Budding fig tree	24:32-35	13:28-31	21:29-33
Faithful servant	24:42-51	13:34-37	12:35-48
Ten virgins	25:1-13		
Talents or minas	25:14-30		19:12-27
Sheep and the goats	25:31-46		

A Friendly Guide to Jesus

Miracles of Jesus

Healing Miracles

Story	Matthew	Mark	Luke	John
Healing Simon Peter's mother-in-law	8:14-15	1:29-31	4:38-39	
Cleansing a leper	8:1-4	1:40-45	5:12-16	
Healing a centurion's servant	8:5-13		7:1-10	
Healing a paralytic	9:1-8	2:1-12	5:17-26	5:2-47
Healing a woman's haemorrhage	9:20-22	5:25-34	8:43-48	
Restoring sight to two blind men	9:27-31 20:29-34			
Restoring a man's withered hand	12:9-14	3:1-6	6:6-11	
Healing a deaf mute		7:31-37		
Giving sight to a blind man at Bethsaida		8:22-26		
Restoring a woman crippled for eighteen years			13:10-17	
Healing a man with dropsy			14:1-6	
Cleansing ten men of leprosy			17:11-19	
Giving sight to a blind man		10:46-52 (Bartimaeus)	18:35-43	9:1-41
Healing a royal official's son at Cana				4:46-54

Restoration Miracles

Story	Matthew	Mark	Luke	John
Raising from the dead a widow's son at Nain			7:11-17	
Raising from the dead the daughter of Jairus	9:18-19,23-26	5:21-24,35-43	8:40-42,49-56	
Raising Lazarus of Bethany from the dead				11:1-44

Nature Miracles

Story	Matthew	Mark	Luke	John
Miraculous catch of fish			5:1-11	21:1-14
Stilling a storm on the Sea of Galilee	8:23-27	4:35-41	8:22-25	
Feeding five thousand people	14:13-21	6:32-44	9:10b-17	6:1-15
Walking on the water	14:22-33	6:45-52		6:16-21
Feeding four thousand people	15:32-38	8:1-10		

Exorcisms (Note: There are no exorcisms in the Gospel of John)

Story	Matthew	Mark	Luke	John
Man with unclean spirit in synagogue at Capernaum		1:23-28	4:33-37	
Gerasene demoniac	8:28-34	5:1-20	8:26-39	
Mute (and blind) demoniac	9:32-34 12:22-30		11:14-15	
Syro-Phoenician woman's daughter	15:21-28	7:24-30		
Boy with an epileptic spirit	17:14-21	9:14-29	9:37-43a	

John 20:30-31 "Jesus did many other miraculous signs in the presence of his disciples, which are not recorded in this book. But these are written that you may believe that Jesus is the Christ, the Son of God, and that by believing you may have life in his name."

It's come back positive: the Annunciation in North Queensland

In many of the pictures of Jan Hynes's paintings in this book there are three similar objects, a reference to the Trinity. Here we see three clipped, potted plants. Mary is wearing a blue dress, the colour associated with spirituality. The ibis is Townsville's dove, the Holy Spirit in the form of a bird.

The fenced garden contains those inside and keeps them pure, protecting them from the evils of the outside world. In Renaissance paintings of the Annunciation, there is often a distinction between the inside world (purity) and the outside world (evil). Walls, fences or garden borders often make a boundary. Here Easter lilies and Christmas lilies make up the border of the garden and are a portent of Jesus' future.

The decoration of the Christmas star alludes to the star of Bethlehem. The Telstra worker in the hang glider is the modern equivalent to the Archangel Gabriel bringing the message of the Annunciation.

3: Stories of Jesus' birth

When you preach sermons regularly, you get some praise and some criticism. The most devastating criticism I received was after a Christmas Day sermon. I was celebrating Mass at a homeless shelter. After the Mass, Jim – a sad-faced man – came up and said, 'I was hoping that your sermon would give me a reason to go on living. But it didn't.' I sympathised with his disappointment, listened to his hard story that made him want to end it all, and then we went down to eat Christmas dinner together.

For Jim, as for many other people, Christmas was a bitterly hard time. The shop windows, presents and cards, Santa Claus, the shepherds and angels gathered around a loving family, reminded him of things he had never had and things from which he had excluded himself. His family was broken, his childhood sad and loveless, the friends he had met on the streets dead, his own family alienated by his drinking, his money gone, and his future more of the same. Christmas, when the streets were full of images of spending, celebration and family, was for him a lonely time.

Jim's life was part of the story. But the sentimental way Christmas is presented was another part of it. The crib is clean, the animals do not smell, the babies always smile, people are happy buying and receiving presents, and families love coming together on Christmas Day. Christmas is for perfect and lucky people. These are the people whom God loves and favours. Their perfect enjoyment of Christmas must make other people feel weak and left out: even God does not really love them.

This way of looking at Christmas and the Christmas stories makes it seem to be about small blessings. It answers our everyday questions about what makes us happy and what our lives are about. But it does not answer our deeper questions. It says that families are very important, that friends to whom we can give and receive presents are also important. A settled background and a home in which to celebrate are important, and so is the ability to spend. These things are certainly blessings. But if they are the deepest blessings, then those, like Jim, who suffer and are lonely would be condemned to be forever unhappy.

The Christmas stories of Jesus, though, cut much deeper than this. They sum up the whole 'Good News' Gospel. The Good News they speak of addresses our deepest questions about the meaning of our lives and world. They speak of a God who loves us in the hardest and most lonely places of our lives. They are about the love of God in a broken world. And they invite us to follow Jesus to the lonely places and people of our world.

The infancy gospels

The stories of Jesus' birth in the Gospels of Matthew and Luke are not sentimental. Here I shall look only at Luke's Gospel. In the section dealing with Jesus' childhood Luke tells us who Jesus is, why he matters, and what this means for our way of living. His stories introduce the large themes of his gospel. You can see this from a summary of the first two chapters.

He tells first how an angel appears to Zechariah to tell him that his wife Elizabeth will have a baby, despite her advanced age. The angel Gabriel then appears to Mary, Elizabeth's cousin, to tell her that she too would also have a child, despite being a virgin. Elizabeth's child is to be called John (the Baptist); Mary's child is to be called Jesus. These stories of Mary and Elizabeth are joined when Mary goes to visit Elizabeth whose child stirs in the womb as Mary greets her. Luke then describes in succession the birth and naming of John the Baptist and the birth and naming of Jesus. The account of Jesus' childhood concludes with short accounts of Jesus being taken to the temple and being recognised as the Messiah by two devout Jews, Simeon and Anna. At the age of twelve Jesus returns to the temple where the teachers of Israel are amazed by his wisdom.

Luke deals with large questions here. He wants to show that both Jesus and John were central in God's work for his people. There were still disciples of John in Luke's day. They knew that Jesus had been a disciple of John who preached that the day of God's coming was close. So Luke wants also to show that John is the messenger who prepares the way for Jesus. Jesus is central in God's work. John leaps in the womb when Jesus comes. The stories tell us, too, that these two births were God's work, not ordinary human events. Elizabeth was very old and Mary was a virgin. Jesus' name, too, which means 'God is with us', shows that we find God and the deepest meaning of our lives in Jesus.

Luke's stories tell us what matters in our lives. It is to pay attention to God in our daily lives and to follow where he leads us. At first Zechariah is fearful and unsure, but eventually he follows the angel's instructions when naming John. Mary replies to Gabriel's invitation with a simple yes. Anna and Simeon, who bless Jesus, have spent their lives waiting for God to come to rule Israel. Their waiting on God and responding generously shows us what human life is all about. So does Jesus himself when he stays in the temple and puts doing God's business above the call of family.

In this gospel Mary is the ideal disciple. She agrees simply to God's invitation. She also pays attention to God in her own life, pondering on the significant events in which she has been involved.

We are also told what Israel can look forward to through Jesus. The rich and mighty will be humbled. He will bring freedom for the little people. The story of Jesus' birth says it all. It is not comfortable. Mary and Joseph have to leave their home town and give birth in the fields. Those invited by God to celebrate it are shepherds, the most disreputable of the rural poor in Jewish society.

> All went to their own towns to be registered. Joseph also went from the town of Nazareth in Galilee to Judea, to the city of David called Bethlehem, because he was descended from the house and family of David. He went to be registered with Mary, to whom he was engaged and who was expecting a child. While they were there, the time came for her to deliver her child. And she gave birth to her firstborn son and wrapped him in bands of cloth, and laid him in a manger, because there was no place for them in the inn.
>
> Luke 2:3–7

Luke describes Jesus' conception as the work of the Holy Spirit. We see that God is powerfully and intimately present in Jesus' life. But the Jews also looked forward to the day of the Lord when the Spirit would be poured out on Israel. So the work of the Spirit in the life of Jesus showed that God's promises to Israel would be realised through him. The Spirit, too, would be present powerfully in his life. The stories of Jesus' birth, though, suggest that God would be present in strange ways.

Luke shows us what we can expect if we follow Jesus. Mary is told that her own soul will be pierced. This violent image hints at the death of Jesus. Mary's future grief is also indicated in her separation from Jesus when he stays behind in the temple. To be a follower of Jesus is to love, and love always includes suffering.

When we look closely at Luke's stories of Jesus' birth and infancy, they are not sentimental stories that are designed to help us feel good and pious. They are strong stories about what matters, about a God in whom we can see the love of God that always reaches out to us at the edges of our lives and society. They invite us to follow Jesus in accompanying people on the edges.

Where the gospels begin

The gospels and St Paul's letters show God to be acting through Jesus' life. Each focuses on the occasion where God first reveals himself as being present in Jesus and where Jesus is seen as being the Son of God. They show the Holy Spirit as being active in these moments.

Paul and the resurrection

In his letters Paul does not tell stories of Jesus' life. He focuses on the meaning of Jesus' death and resurrection. We see clearly that God has been active in Jesus' rising from the dead. Jesus is shown then to be the Son of God. So in his Letter to the Romans St Paul speaks of the

> gospel concerning his Son who was descended from David according to the flesh and was declared to be Son of God with power according to the Spirit of holiness by resurrection from the dead… (Romans 1:3–4)

Gospel of Mark

In Mark's Gospel we first meet Jesus when he is baptised by John the Baptist. When he is baptised, the heavens open, the Spirit descends like a dove on him, and a voice from heaven says 'You are my Son, the beloved'. So Jesus is shown to be the Son of God at the beginning of his preaching of the Gospel.

Gospels of Matthew and Luke

The Gospels of Matthew and Luke both show God acting in Jesus at the very beginning of his life. An angel says to Mary 'The Holy Spirit will come upon you…and therefore the child to be born will be holy; he will be called Son of God'. In Matthew's Gospel, the angel tells Joseph that Mary will bear a son and that he is to be called Jesus. This name means 'God is with us'. So the story of Jesus' childhood tells us that Jesus is the creation of the Spirit and reveals God working in him.

The fourth gospel

The opening of the fourth gospel takes us back before Jesus' birth. It describes Jesus as the word of God who was with God from the beginning, and was at work in the creation of the world. Jesus was in God's plan for humanity from eternity.

The importance of Jesus

The stories of Jesus' childhood are not simply affectionate memories preserved by his relatives. In them the gospel writers tell us that Jesus matters because of his intimate relationship to God.

The elders sit down and listen

This picture is set on the steps of the Sacred Heart Cathedral in Townsville and features identities of the local community (radio announcer, mayor, Evelyn Scott – who was chairperson for the Reconciliation Council – and representatives from education and the military services). Bishop Michael Putney sits at the top of the steps at the closed door of the Cathedral.

On the left is an apple tree, symbolising the fruit tree in the Garden of Eden in the Book of Genesis, and on the right is a palm tree, symbolising resurrection in the New Testament.

Jesus, the boy in the foreground, wears white, symbolising purity and innocence. His T-shirt features blue stars, which could suggest the emblem of the Eureka flag or the Star of David. The boy wears a baseball cap typical of many skateboarding youth, but could also be a yarmulke worn by males of the Jewish faith, of which Jesus was one. His skateboard is decorated with the Australian Aboriginal flag, suggesting that non-Indigenous Australian residents have much to learn from Indigenous culture

4: Jesus with people

Among my most vivid early memories is the first day of each school year. We all wondered what the new teacher would be like. The imagination ran riot, ranging from a kindly face – a school boy's paradise – to a fearsome tyrant imposing a reign of terror. The excitement and anxiety peaked as the bell rang for the first class, and we waited for the new master to enter the classroom. Forty eyes were fixed on him looking for clues as to what he and the school year would be like.

I have even more raw memories of the days before I went into the classroom to take my first lesson. How should I present myself to those forty beady eyes fixed on me looking for any weakness. There was no shortage of advice. Don't smile before Easter! Make an example of the first student who misbehaves! Don't talk but get the students working straight away! Of course, I learned only from my mistakes.

This first meeting between teacher and students, all this advice, was about more than a single day in the classroom. The way teachers presented themselves and the relationship they established with the students defined for both students and teachers what it meant to learn. It displayed the face of education. In the teacher's face and behaviour students learned whether education was controlling or cooperative, brutal or kindly, humane or impersonal, encouraging or daunting. A lot hung on that first day. The conversation in the playground at the morning break sounded like gossip, but it really touched on the big questions of students' lives and the hopes and fears they had for themselves.

The excitement of the first day at school helps us enter the gospel stories about Jesus' years of teaching and preaching. The Jewish people were like students at the start of the school year. They sensed that something new was coming. People had tried to rebel against the Romans. Some were expecting a great leader who would deliver them. Others waited on God while being faithful to the detailed rules for daily life found in their scriptures. So when anyone came who claimed to speak for God people would listen attentively. They would also look carefully at how they behaved to see what kind of a God, what kind of a message and what kind of a future was expressed in what the speakers did and how they related to people.

So the gospel stories of Jesus' conversations and preaching pay careful attention to what Jesus does as well as what he says. They also notice the reactions of different groups: the Pharisees, Sadducees, the ordinary people and outsiders. Even the smallest story and the smallest gesture are really about big things: who God is, what Israel and the early Christians could hope for, how to live, and about our place in the world.

Jesus' public life

In the gospels Jesus rarely answers directly all the questions that people were asking. He uses images. They appeal to our imagination and make us ask new, better questions. Jesus' teaching and life can be seen as an attempt to expand our imagination.

Jesus' hearers wanted to know whether God would act soon and decisively for Israel. Jesus excites them by speaking of God's kingdom and by saying that it is near. This message focuses people's minds on God's kingdom. They become attentive. They, and we, start asking questions. Does Jesus mean that the kingdom is present but we cannot see it? Does he mean that it is coming soon? Is the kingdom the end of the present world? Or is it a makeover of our present world? What will it mean for us?

Jesus does not answer these questions. He simply gives us different glimpses of what it might look like if we allowed God to rule our lives by following Jesus. The kingdom of God is like seed thrown over a field. It is like a basketful of fish, good and bad. It is like finding a pearl and wanting it so much that you sell everything to possess it. The kingdom of God comes like a thief in the night. It is like a wedding banquet to which we are all invited, but for which we need to stay awake.

Through all these images Jesus points to a reality that is mysterious, attractive and elusive, but is there to be grasped if we attend to it. The way we attend to the kingdom is by attending to Jesus. God is acting decisively in the world through Jesus and we can recognise the signs as long as we keep our eyes and ears open and if we expect to find God being active in our world.

Jesus brings out the importance of God's invitation and closeness to us through images of judgment. The blessings awaiting those who respond faithfully and the doom awaiting those who are careless stress how important it is to respond to the Good News that Jesus preaches. He urges his hearers to go beyond the daily questions of how to survive from day to day and how to make their way in the world. He invites them to attend to the deep questions of where God is to be found in the world and where God is inviting them to go.

Jesus points most vividly to the kingdom through his actions. They gave authority and depth to his words. His actions allowed people to see God in action. For his hearers it was a surprising God.

The actions we associate most strongly with Jesus are miracles. Wonder workers were not uncommon in Jesus' time. Jesus' miracles are distinctive because their message is more important than their power. They tell us what God is like. Jesus drove out the demons and illnesses that sapped peoples' lives and freedom. God was a God of freedom. Jesus enabled blind people to see and deaf people to hear, showing that God could open our eyes and ears to see our world rightly. Jesus cured the lame and helped them to walk freely. God wants us to live fully. Through his miracles Jesus fulfilled the promises that were made to Israel, and showed that in God lay the answers to our big questions.

Luke described Jesus as filled with the Holy Spirit. Miracles show the power of the Spirit at work in him. They also showed what God's promises looked like – healing, freedom and acceptance. People responded to Jesus' words because they were authoritative and spoken with the power of the Spirit.

Jesus' most striking actions were not his miracles but the way he behaved with people. In his relationships he showed what the God of Israel was like. So he cured people on the Sabbath to show what God wanted on God's day. He forgave sins. He saved the life of the woman caught in adultery, refused to condemn her, and blessed her as she went away. He ate with prostitutes and extortionists. These actions were deeply offensive to the Pharisees, because they believed that God cared only for the faithful, and that we should eat only with the people whom God loved. Jesus showed that God wanted the company of sinners. The kingdom of God was for them too.

The God whom people saw in the face and actions of Jesus was surprising, exhilarating and urgent. Jesus' words called them to attend to God's presence in all the people they met and in every situation in which they found themselves. His words still call us to do the same today.

> When he came to Nazareth, where he had been brought up, he went to the synagogue on the sabbath day, as was his custom. He stood up to read, and the scroll of the prophet Isaiah was given to him. He unrolled the scroll and found the place where it was written:
>
> 'The Spirit of the Lord is upon me,
> because he has anointed me
> to bring good news to the poor.
> He has sent me to proclaim release to the captives and recovery of sight to the blind, to let the oppressed go free,
> to proclaim the year of the Lord's favour.'
>
> And he rolled up the scroll, gave it back to the attendant, and sat down. The eyes of all in the synagogue were fixed on him. Then he began to say to them, 'Today this scripture has been fulfilled in your hearing.' All spoke well of him and were amazed at the gracious words that came from his mouth.
>
> Luke 4:16–22

Palestine in Jesus' time

The gospels refer to many groups in Palestine who were part of Jesus' life. The most important were the Romans, the Sadducees and the Pharisees.

The Romans

In Jesus' time Palestine was under Roman rule. Roman representative Pontius Pilate made the important decisions. The Romans had a small garrison in Palestine, but relied on local rulers such as Herod to keep the daily peace. The Romans generally respected Jewish religious traditions, but many Jews thought that their rule contradicted God's promises. They looked to the day when God would free Israel. The occasional rebellions were savagely put down.

The Sadducees

The Sadducees included the high priestly families responsible for worship in the temple. The temple was central to the Jewish economy, and the Sadducees were responsible for keeping order in Jerusalem. When non-Jewish rulers put pressure on the people of Israel to accept their forms of worship and culture, the high priests of the temple and their caste would strive to reach a compromise with the regime.

The Pharisees

The Pharisees began as a protest movement at a time when the Jews were under pressure to compromise in their faith and practice. The Pharisees insisted on being faithful to God by following the Law in all the details of daily life. This was a very generous way of life that could become narrow. Jesus came into conflict with them in his teaching about God's acceptance of sinners. After the Romans destroyed the temple, the Pharisees became dominant in Jewish life. When Christians were separating from Jews in their religious outlook, there was hostility between the two groups. The treatment of the Pharisees in the gospels reflects this.

Washing the feet

This picture is located on The Strand, Townsville's most popular outdoor meeting place for families and friends. It is late afternoon and shadows have darkened the lawn, indicating there are dark times ahead. It is twilight; the sun is setting; the day is closing. Jesus' life on earth is nearing its end.

Jesus is washing the feet of the disciples. The red basin, containing water, alludes to Jesus' blood that will wash away the sins of the world.

Water imagery is prominent in this picture. Water has a cleansing quality, both physically and metaphorically. Jesus is referred to as life-giving water. Between the group of people and the island in the background is the sea, a body of water which would wash clean anyone crossing to the island, a symbol for life beyond this world.

Judas is absent, represented by an empty red chair, alluding to the blood of Christ which will be poured out for the forgiveness of all sins, including Judas's sins. The other chairs are blue.

The empty shoes are open to interpretation by the viewer.

5: The invitation to follow Jesus

I never mind being criticised by people for being too radical. It is a compliment in a way – after all, Jesus was radical. But if I am forced to compare myself with someone who lives out the Gospel more radically than I do, that is painful.

Once I was preaching in a struggling suburban parish. The Gospel told the story of a rich young man whom Jesus invited to sell everything that he had and to follow Jesus. When the young man went away sad, Jesus remarks that it is harder for a rich man to enter the kingdom of God than for a camel to pass through the eye of a needle.

I told the congregation that this gospel story did not mean that we had literally to sell all that we had, and that the bit about the camel and the needle was a strong image not to be taken literally. We could follow Jesus by living ordinary, generous lives.

After Mass a couple came up to me and said how much they were moved to hear this gospel story read. It had inspired them to sell their property in Perth, move to Melbourne and to work with people addicted to drugs.

I thought again about what I had said. Had I made the story of the rich young man too soft? Did I take the following of Jesus seriously enough? Who had understood the story better – I, or the couple who had staked their property and their future on it? Of course, I had other thoughts too. Were the couple prudent? Would their commitment to help people with drugs be sustainable? Would their energy burn out under the pressure of hard reality, and make them disillusioned? But, I thought, Jesus surely would not let them down.

So I was left with the question that the Gospel invites us all to ask: What does it mean to follow Jesus and to be his disciple? The gospel stories of Jesus are very radical and even uncomfortable. In the gospels, too, no one ever gets it quite right. Some people regard what Jesus says as nonsense. Others, like the rich young man, find it all too hard. Some, like Peter, commit themselves boldly, but go missing when the path along which Jesus invites them becomes too steep. Some make compromises – they follow Jesus but only by night. Or they want to sell their oxen and settle things at home first. In the gospel stories Jesus invites us to follow him like his disciples. Like them, we are weak and make compromises. But as we follow Jesus through the stories told about him we continually find ourselves asking how God would like us to live as Jesus' disciples.

Jesus and discipleship

Each gospel has its own way of describing what it means to be a disciple of Jesus. Mark describes being a disciple as like walking along a path. If we are disciples, we follow closely behind him. If we are afraid or simply interested in him, we are further away from him. John describes being a disciple as like looking at Jesus and hearing him. Matthew describes the disciple as a person who obeys God's law of love.

All the gospels suggest that if we are disciples we shall make Jesus the centre of our lives. We find in him the way to answer all the large questions of our lives, and also discover how we are to live. We don't follow Jesus because he is a good bloke, but because we recognise that God is present in him. Because he is at the centre of our lives, being a disciple is full on. We can't put a bet each way on it.

Being a disciple also takes us further than we would think of going. Jesus says that if we want to be his disciples we must take up our cross and follow him. He insists that we must want to be ready to do and to suffer whatever lies on our way.

Being a disciple also runs against everything we usually associate with being successful. We are to respond patiently when provoked, to put no weight on possessions and security, to serve simply rather than to have positions of power, to choose the company of the disreputable rather than the movers and shakers in society, and not to seek to be noticed or to be a celebrity.

If we are to be as radical as this in our readiness to go wherever Jesus takes us, and to treat so lightly what people value highly, our hearts must be caught by a great vision. Jesus must capture our imagination with a dream of what our life and world could be like. In the gospels, Jesus expands our imagination by the stories that he tells. They are big stories about big gestures. The Samaritan stops to pick up and care for his traditional enemy. A man is forced to walk one mile by his oppressor, and then willingly goes another mile with him. A merchant finds a rare pearl and sells everything he owns to possess it. A king invites the beggars at the market to the marriage of his son.

Behind these stories is a God who is as 'stir-crazy' as the disciple is invited to be. Disciples are to be overwhelmed by God's love for us, and God's love is shown in his sending his Son to die so painfully for us. Love is infectious, so we are attracted to follow Jesus in giving our lives generously for others.

The Spirit of God helps us to understand Jesus' path, and gives us courage to speak of him and to model our lives on him. The Spirit gives energy and intimacy to our relationship with Jesus, and enables us to respond to God's love.

Because love cannot be measured, neither can discipleship. In Mark's Gospel, in particular, the disciples love enough to want to follow Jesus. But they constantly let him down. Following Jesus is like a game of snakes and ladders. For every ladder we climb, a snake of weakness or stupidity takes us down again. But because God loves us, we are always invited to climb again. If we want to love God and one another, we are still 'in play' as disciples.

Being a disciple means that our heart is captured by Jesus, that we have a big heart, an ordinary human capacity for weakness and betrayal, and a big desire to love as we are loved.

> As he was setting out on a journey, a man ran up and knelt before him, and asked him, 'Good Teacher, what must I do to inherit eternal life?' Jesus said to him, 'Why do you call me good? No one is good but God alone. You know the commandments: "You shall not murder; You shall not commit adultery; You shall not steal; You shall not bear false witness; You shall not defraud; Honour your father and mother." ' He said to him, 'Teacher, I have kept all these since my youth.' Jesus, looking at him, loved him and said, 'You lack one thing; go, sell what you own, and give the money to the poor, and you will have treasure in heaven; then come, follow me.' When he heard this, he was shocked and went away grieving, for he had many possessions.
>
> Mark 10:17–22

Followers of Jesus

All Christians are called to follow Christ, which always involves recognising what matters and living by it. At different times distinctive forms of 'following' have been most encouraging to people. Here are four examples.

Polycarp the martyr (died 155 CE)

Polycarp was Bishop of Smyrna, a rich town in present-day Turkey. He is said to have known John the apostle. In his late eighties he was killed in a time of persecution. The story of his death shows martyrdom to be the perfect way to follow Jesus. As in the story of Jesus, Polycarp was taken into the city on a donkey; he answered the Governor calmly, and the crowd demanded his execution. When he was stabbed to death on a fire, blood poured out and a dove, the symbol of the Holy Spirit, flew out. He was not only a renowned teacher but an incomparable martyr. He inspired Christians of his time to want to imitate him in his martyrdom because it so perfectly illustrated the example of Jesus in the gospels.

Antony the hermit (died 350 CE)

Antony lived in Egypt towards the end of the great persecutions. His parents died when he was a young man. Soon after, he heard the message in the Gospel passage that tells us to leave all and follow Jesus. He sold all he had, and went first to the graveyards to pray and wrestle with demons. He was then led to go into the desert, where he lived and prayed in an old Roman fort for many years. His fame spread, and soon pilgrims came to ask him for advice and to seek favours from him. Many people wanted to share his way of life, and monasteries sprang up in the desert. This life of prayer and total focus on God reminded people of what mattered, and encouraged them in their own lives.

Hildegard the teacher (died 1179 CE)

Hildegard lived by the Rhine valley in Germany. From her childhood she was attached to a church, living a life of solitary prayer there. People heard of her and came to share her way of life. Elected prioress, she overcame great resistance in moving her community to Bingen. She became notable for her visions, her learning and her musical skills. Her chaplains and bishop attested to their authenticity. She spent much time travelling, preaching and giving advice to people all along the Rhine valley. She has inspired many women to have a public role within the Catholic Church.

Dorothy Day the peacemaker (died 1980 CE)

Dorothy Day was a politically radical student in the United States. When she moved to New York, she spent time in gaol, wrote for socialist newspapers, had an abortion, married and was divorced. She became a Catholic, but in her new life she at first missed the passion for justice that Communists had showed. She then met Peter Maurin, a radical French Catholic, whose ideas of following Jesus inspired her. She founded a weekly newspaper, the *Catholic Worker*, which was dedicated to social justice and to pacifism, and formed open communities where the poor could live as equals. She was jailed many times, and lost most of her readers when the *Catholic Worker* opposed the civil war in Spain and the use of nuclear weapons on Japan. She inspired and was a spiritual guide to many people who wanted to live the Gospel wholeheartedly.

The burial

This picture is set in Townsville's old West End Cemetery with Castle Hill in the background. Castle Hill dominates the city of Townsville and in the series of paintings in this book represents Calvary, or perhaps the mountain to which we lift our eyes, or the 'light' on the top of the hill.

The light is fading and the body has to be buried before sundown, according to Jewish tradition.

The cross, the headstone of the grave, is a reminder of Christ's recent crucifixion as well as the future symbol of Christianity.

The men, Joseph of Arimathea and Nicodemus, lower the body into the grave. Shaven heads indicate lamentation.

The women, the two Marys, want to be there, but are holding back. Mary the mother of Jesus and Mary Magdalene approach the grave slowly, comforting each other although almost paralysed with grief. The gestures of the two women are significant. The mother of Jesus covers her eyes, a protective gesture as though not wanting to see what is before her. Mary Magdalene touches her heart, a gesture indicating her connection with Jesus was of the heart.

The ibis, representing the Holy Spirit, is about to ascend from the body of Jesus. The ibis is a bird with significant meaning in many cultures. The Greeks identified the ibis with Hermes, messenger of the Gods. In Townsville the ibis is one of the most common birds, a constant presence and reminder.

The seedling represents new life, the resurrection, which is soon to take place. Three leaves allude to the Trinity, new life and new hope.

Each year Easter's placement on the calendar is determined by the cycle of the moon. The phases of the moon – full moon, new moon and the stages in-between – remind us of the transitory nature of life. The moon rising in the evening sky alerts us to the connection of Easter with a full moon.

On the headstone a bottle of aftershave or body perfume, similar to what a young man might use today, replaces the expensive oils and perfume of olden times. This is a reference to the expensive herbs used to preserve the body of Jesus. The spades on either side of the grave suggest work that has been done (digging the grave) and work yet to be done (filling in the grave). It is also a metaphor for the foundation of the Christian Church.

6: Jesus' death

One of the most disturbing and moving ceremonies I have been involved in was a baptism at a detention centre. We chaplains would not normally baptise people in detention because there was no Christian community there to which they could belong. But we did baptise Yousuf when the Australian Government was preparing to send him back to his homeland.

He had fled to Australia because he wanted to become a Christian, but his claim for protection here had been rejected. He was sure that when he was sent back to his own country he would be tortured and killed if he lived his Christian faith publicly. So he asked to be baptised to strengthen him for the torture and death that awaited him. His fear was real and seemed justified. So we agreed to baptise him.

I was deeply moved by Yousuf's bravery. He had asked himself what mattered most deeply in his life. He had found the answer in Jesus. That had led him to come to Australia. But now he faced a more agonising question: If Jesus was the answer to the big questions of his life, how could he make sense of the pain, humiliation and brutal death he feared? How could he bear these things?

I had my own questions to answer. I was disturbed by my part in the baptism. In it I represented two communities. I represented the community of Christ's followers that welcomed Yousuf into the new life that baptism brings through Jesus' death. I also represented the Australian community, which was sending Yousuf away to, as he saw it, his own death. I was an agent of life and of death.

I too had to ask again what mattered most deeply to me. How did I respond as a fellow human being and fellow Christian to this man who was being sent from my country in fear of a terrible fate? How did I respond to my suspicion that the Australian community, whose privileges I enjoyed, was sending an innocent man to torture and death? In his shoes, would I have chosen to die rather than keep my faith a merely private thing? Or did my life and security matter more to me than my faith? Ultimately, how much did Yousuf's life and death matter to me? How much did our shared faith matter to me?

We both had to ask big and seemingly unanswerable questions. His questions were matters of life and death. Mine were less costly, at least in the short term. But they all went to the heart of what it means to be human, and of what it means to suffer.

We Christians have always looked for the meaning of suffering and catastrophe in the death of Jesus on the cross. At first sight our faith seems only to explain the meaning of one disaster by telling the story of a worse one. So why is Jesus' death the place where we might find our questions about suffering answered and guidance on how to live in the face of it?

Finding meaning in Jesus' death

In the stories of Jesus' death all the things that ordinarily give meaning and happiness to our lives are stripped away from him. As Australian citizens we take for granted our freedom, our personal safety and dignity, and the protection that the law gives us. But if we were to speak to any asylum seeker, we would hear how misery and anxiety could quickly come upon us if we were deprived of these things. At the end of his life Jesus is arrested, imprisoned, condemned in a rigged trial, rejected by the crowd, tortured and killed in a way designed to remove his human dignity.

As persons we find meaning in the love and support of our friends, the respect of our acquaintances, and in the confidence that what we believe in is right. Jesus is rejected by his people, betrayed by one friend, denied by another, and deserted by the rest. Dying, he feels abandoned by the God to whom he committed his life.

Jesus' death tested everything that mattered to him, as it would test us. There is no depth of abandonment to which we could go that Jesus has not already reached.

Ultimately, it was sin that tested Jesus' faith. The sins of many people conspired to isolate him and strip him of that which gave his life meaning. But sin did not succeed. The fear of Pilate, the ambition and cynicism of the high priests, the narrowness of the Pharisees, the cowardice of Peter, the greed of Judas and the fickleness of the ordinary people meant that he had to die painfully, alone and unsupported.

Jesus had to wrestle with the thought that a generous life in which he had trusted God as Father had led him to be isolated, rejected, beaten, tortured, killed and maybe even abandoned by God ('Why have you forsaken me?' he cries). In his place we might be tempted to conclude that sin, which does such terrible things, is stronger than goodness and faithfulness. We might even reach the point at which we wonder if we were right about what really matters, or whether we should listen to our fear that tells us to walk away from our faith.

If Jesus' death tests faith so terribly, it might seem surprising that the gospels make us focus on his death. Why don't they let us forget about Jesus' death, and invite us look somewhere else to find meaning in our lives?

The reason for this is that the early Christians had discovered that Jesus had risen from the dead. At a time when their own faith had been shattered, they recognised the risen Jesus, found him as their companion, and experienced his power. In the light of this life-changing experience, they now recognised that Jesus' death was the place where sin had been overcome and where God's love was shown. Jesus' way to death was our way to live fully. They did not explain how this was so, but tried to expand our imagination.

They did this by showing how Jesus' death fitted with the great points of their history in which they had found the meaning of their lives, and particularly with their rescue from slavery in Egypt. They saw Jesus as being like the sacrificial lamb that was eaten at the Passover meal. Before they left Egypt the Jews sprinkled the sacrificed lamb's blood on their doorsteps. It protected them from plague. So Jesus' blood was a protection. Jesus was also the promised servant whose sufferings freed the people. His obedience healed our disobedience.

> When it was noon, darkness came over the whole land until three in the afternoon. At three o'clock Jesus cried out with a loud voice, 'Eloi, Eloi, lema sabachthani?' which means, 'My God, my God, why have you forsaken me?'
>
> Mark 15:33–34

John's Gospel pictures Jesus' death as the point when the promised Spirit came. When Jesus died, he gave up his Spirit. The place that we associate with being cursed – because Jesus died there – is the place where promise and blessing – in the form of the Holy Spirit – are born and began to spread through the world.

Jesus' death took him to the most terrible places to which a human being could go and to the most terrible things human beings can do to one another. But in his death God's love overcame all of humanity's hatred and apathy. As Paul said later, Jesus' death showed us that despite all our fears and anxieties 'nothing can separate us from God's love for us made visible in Christ'.

For disciples of Jesus this knowledge gives us confidence and strength in following his way. We know that it will lead us through suffering. But this is a way of life, not a cause for leaving our path. We discover on this path what really matters.

Why was Jesus killed?

The New Testament tells us that Jesus' death matters because it is the centre of God's plan for us. The gospel stories are full of references to the Old Testament which illustrate the meaning of Jesus' death. They are not stories of the kind we might find from a modern journalist. They tell us why Jesus died for us. If we want to know why different people wanted him dead and how they planned to have him killed, we need to consider the different groups of Jesus' day.

The Romans
The Roman authorities were directly responsible for Jesus' death. Only Pontius Pilate, the Roman governor, could have someone crucified. Crucifixion was the penalty for plotting against Roman rule. Pilate may have been convinced that Jesus was dangerous because he was described as the promised king who would set Israel free. Pilate would have understood this as a political claim. However, the gospels downplay Pilate's responsibility because the position of Christians in the Roman empire was precarious at best rather than a threat to the authorities. If the gospels had wanted to emphasise Pilate's responsibility, they would have had to explain why a Roman governor executed Jesus for treason. They did not do this.

The high priests
Different groups of Jews also had reasons for wanting Jesus dead. The Jewish authorities – the high priests and their council – would have feared his popularity and the claim that he was the Messiah. This threatened the peace of the city and therefore invited Roman intervention. When Jesus drove sellers out of the temple, this could have been the last straw. The temple and the trade associated with it were the centre of Jerusalem's economy. So it would have been logical for those in charge of the temple to have plotted to have Jesus killed by handing him over to Pilate.

The Pharisees
The gospels describe Jesus' conflicts with the Pharisees that led them to hate him. Their hostility became increasingly murderous. Jesus and the Pharisees had different understandings of how God mattered, and what God asks us to do. The Pharisees may have aroused the crowds to turn against Jesus, but they were not powerful enough to have him brought to trial.

The Jewish people
The Gospels of Matthew and John give a significant place to the Jewish people. Pilate is afraid of the crowd, wants to release Jesus, but the crowd demands his death. The crowd is portrayed as representing the Jewish people in their rejection of Jesus. But the people in the crowd were not responsible for Jesus' death. They were unlikely to have terrorised such a hard man as Pilate was reputed to have been. Angry crowds represent humanity at its most sinful and selfish, not a nation of people. The significance of 'the crowd' is that it is made up of people like us, and it is people like us who would applaud Jesus' death.

Visiting the grave

This picture takes place in the same location as that which was seen in *The Burial* picture. But it is now the next day. The concreter has sealed the grave and is about to leave the scene. The grave is guarded by armed soldiers wearing tropical fatigues from the defence force based in Townsville.

There are floral tributes on the grave: lilies and holly. Lilies mean purity and sacredness, and make an appropriate statement about Jesus. Lilies in Jan Hynes's paintings can be Christmas lilies, Easter lilies or both, thus representing Christ as the alpha and the omega, the beginning and the end. Holly, being red, is associated with the blood of the crucifixion. Being circular in shape, the holly wreath has no beginning or end, and represents eternity. The holly wreath today is commonly used as a Christmas decoration. The depiction of the floral tributes encompasses the news of the coming of Jesus' birth, his death and his resurrection.

The grave decorations on the graves either side of Jesus' grave are significant. They are both meant to be small statues of hands in prayer. The broken and fallen hands on the left symbolise one who has not repented for his sins whereas the hands on the right are in a prayerful pose and symbolise one who has repented and is being redeemed. These grave decorations refer to the two thieves who were crucified along with Christ – one chose to accept Jesus as the Son of God; the other did not.

The plants at the foot of the graves reinforce the notion of the two thieves and the choices they made (to be unrepentant and die, or to repent and have eternal life). There is wheat growing from a crevice in the grave on the left, but it is not in 'good soil' and cannot flourish, so it withers and will die. This is also a reference to the parable of the sower. On the right we see the outcome of the seed that fell on fertile ground; it flourishes and has three branches, a reference to the Trinity.

Mary, the mother of Jesus, kneels at the graveside, handkerchief in hand, and mourns for her son. Mary Magdalene stands back, a little uncertain with her head bowed in a forlorn pose and mourns for Jesus. She carries a bunch of roses, a modern-day symbol of love. Red roses also represent the resurrection: the thorns signify pain, the red colour signifies blood, and the sweet perfume of roses signifies the afterlife.

The ibis as the Holy Spirit ascends toward heaven, alluding to the resurrection of Christ.

7: Jesus' rising from the dead

One of the most riveting events on television in 2009 was the inauguration of Barack Obama as President of the United States of America. But the centre of attention was not the new President but the people who had come to Washington. Particularly the Black Americans who had come from all states of the union.

They spoke simply and powerfully about what the inauguration meant to them and why they had come to Washington for it. For all of them it was something that they had never expected to see.

They told stories. One woman had come to represent her grandmother who grew up prevented from sitting on the same seats as white people, and would never have believed this day possible. An old man who had been with Martin Luther King as he struggled for desegregation said he had longed for the day when he would see a black president. But he never thought that he would see one in his lifetime.

As an Australian, I was reminded of our Parliamentary Apology to Indigenous Australians a year earlier. Indigenous Australians spoke of their long journey and of their joy that so much discrimination and dismissal had ended in this day of reconciliation.

What was distinctive about the American Black speakers was how naturally they spoke of their own story in the language and images of scripture. They had been on a long journey. Like the Israelites who wandered through the desert for forty years, they could see this day as their entry into the promised land.

The hopes they had in their journey were now fulfilled. Of course the journey would go on after Obama, after the Apology, but this day was special. It gave them new hope in their living.

These events and the response of those who were present at them recall the impact that Jesus' rising from the dead must have had on his followers. They had followed him and lost their hope when he was crucified. But when they met the risen Jesus, they saw their journey in a new way and understood what it meant to follow him.

Finding meaning in Jesus' rising

Jesus rises from the dead at the end of his life. But for his followers it was the beginning of their faith. They saw him in a new way and recognised that he was the key to the long history of God's relationship with Israel. They found in him the key to answering their large questions and saw more clearly what following him meant.

They had seen Jesus through the lens of the promises God had made to Israel. When he rose from the dead, they saw those promises in a fresh way. They recognised that God had fulfilled those promises. How does Jesus' resurrection fulfil the promises made to Israel and answer our deep questions?

Our deepest question is whether we and our lives matter at all. Death puts that question to us because all we have done, all our relationships and all our projects in this world come to an end. Our own death also makes us wonder about the larger things in which we find meaning – whether God is real and whether the struggle to leave the world a better place is really worth it. For the disciples Jesus' death called into question everything that God had promised through the prophets to Israel.

Jesus' rising from the dead answered all those questions without the need for words. It showed that death did not have the last word. Death did not mean the end of our existence or of our relationships. It did not say that our life's work was futile. Jesus came back to give joy to his friends, and invited them to continue his work.

Jesus' rising from the dead also showed that, despite the disciples' fears after Jesus' death, all that he had spoken about God's promises was true. God had remained faithful to his promises. They saw the resurrection of Jesus through the lens of God's promises.

Seen from that perspective Jesus' rising from the dead speaks to us in the same way as it spoke to the disciples. It addresses the questions that death puts to us. We can be anxious when we ask what really matters, because it makes us wonder whether we ourselves really matter. If we believe that our existence ends with our death, then that question is sharper – particularly if our life's project has ended in failure and our life in rejection. But to know that death is not the end, and that someone who was locked out of the world by being killed still lives is very reassuring. It says that death and failure are not necessarily the end of things, and that our life matters more than our experience often suggests.

But for the early Christians the resurrection also spoke to all the other hopes they had. If they hoped for freedom, the greatest freedom was to know that those whom they loved would live happily with God after death. If they hoped for connection, the joy that Jesus gave the disciples suggested that the end of life was not about isolation, but about joining those we love in new ways. If they hoped for a just world, they found confidence that God shared their passion and that what we built here would endure in the next life. If they looked for a meaning to life, they found a God who made us out of love, joined us in love in Jesus, and is with us in our journey out of this world to the rich and happy risen life that Jesus lived. Jesus' rising from the dead was a symbol of all of their hopes – and ours.

> As they came near the village to which they were going, he walked ahead as if he were going on. But they urged him strongly, saying, 'Stay with us, because it is almost evening and the day is now nearly over.' So he went in to stay with them. When he was at the table with them, he took bread, blessed and broke it, and gave it to them. Then their eyes were opened, and they recognized him; and he vanished from their sight. They said to each other, 'Were not our hearts burning within us while he was talking to us on the road, while he was opening the scriptures to us?' That same hour they got up and returned to Jerusalem; and they found the eleven and their companions gathered together.
>
> Luke 24:28–33

In the gospel stories there is no attempt to say what Jesus' rising is like. They do not describe it or explain how it happens. People meet the risen Jesus, and the meetings are always both domestic and extraordinary. Jesus is with them in rooms and eats fish with them. But he comes through locked doors, is sometimes recognised and sometimes not.

It would be foolish, then, to try to analyse what happened in Jesus' resurrection or to imagine that we could have photographed it if we had been in the tomb where his body lay. It is important, too, that the resurrection be more than we could ever understand. If we could analyse and explain it, it would be the answer only to the small questions which we ask, not to the large questions.

The stories in the gospels are not about explaining. As always, they are about expanding our imagination. They encourage us to hope larger hopes for ourselves and our world, and to see Jesus as the one who fulfils those hopes. They show what the risen Jesus means for us if we believe and trust in him.

Images of the resurrection

The New Testament never described how the resurrection of Jesus happened. It was seen as something that God did, full of mystery and understood only by those of the faith.

But even if the New Testament writers did not describe the resurrection, they did describe its effects. After the resurrection, the tomb was empty and Jesus appeared to his disciples.

Appearances of Jesus

Paul's is the earliest account of the resurrection. Repeating what he has been taught, he says that Christ

> was raised on the third day in accordance with the scriptures, and that he appeared to Cephas, then to the twelve. Then he appeared to more than five hundred brothers and sisters at one time, most of whom are still alive, though some have died. Then he appeared to James, then to all the apostles. (1 Corinthians 15:4–7)

The gospels include many stories of Jesus appearing to his disciples. Jesus eats with them and displays his wounds to show that he is not a ghost. But his appearing is always mysterious. He comes into locked rooms, is not recognised at first, arouses the kind of terror associated with God's presence, and appears only to people to whom he matters. To see him is a deep spiritual experience that changes people's lives.

The empty tomb

The gospels, too, describe the disciples finding the tomb empty. It is a mysterious event. They have a vision of angels who explain the significance of the empty tomb to them: Jesus is risen. Like the holy place in the temple, the tomb is seen as a place of wonder where God's power is at work.

Mark's Gospel probably first ended with the women's discovery of the empty tomb, and the angel's instruction to tell the apostles to go to Galilee where they would see Jesus. But the women are too afraid to tell them. So this gospel ends in the deep mystery that God's presence is stronger than our resistance.

In the other gospels, the finding of the empty tomb leads to appearances of Jesus where the joy and mystery of his rising from the dead are spelled out.

Adoration on The Strand

Joseph (wearing his carpenter's clothes), Mary (once again in blue representing spirituality) and Jesus stroll on The Strand as many families do. Jesus is in his stroller and has hands stretched out, portending his position on the cross. His stroller has a canopy, which is suggestive of a throne seen in many religious paintings. It is decorated with a star (a reference to the Star of Bethlehem and the Star of David).

The Magi are wearing the doctoral gowns of James Cook University and adopt the traditional poses commonly found in paintings of The Adoration. The first is kneeling with hat removed and head well bowed; the second stands, holding her hat with head partially bowed; and the third stands tall, wearing her hat. There is a transition of footwear from closed-in shoes, to sandals, to bare feet.

The third Magi is Dr Evelyn Scott, founding chairperson of the Reconciliation Council, recognised by the black hat she always wore and the black academic gown with a red border (a reference to black skin and red blood).

There are three gifts offered to the baby Jesus. The emu egg represents birth; a toy lamb represents the Lamb of God, the Golden Fleece of Greek legend, and Australia in its earlier history of agricultural affluence, riding on the back of the 'golden fleece'; and a boomerang represents the resurrection, the return of life.

On the left of the picture is a coastal almond tree recognisable by the characteristic way the branches grow out horizontally (like a cross), and its bright red leaves. The red leaves are in the position of the wounds of the stigmata (hands, side and feet).

On the right of the picture is a palm tree, its branches radiating upwards, symbolic of the resurrection.

The light source in the foreground represents the light of the world.

The Holy Spirit this time is represented by a red-tailed black cockatoo.

8: The Son of God

When people give up on faith, they often do so after they have suffered terribly. That was so with Agnes. She had been raised in a devout family, attended Mass regularly and seemed a 'rusted-on' Catholic. Then her daughter caught leukaemia from which she later died. Her mother died soon afterwards in a road accident. In her grief and her anger she stopped going to church and lost her belief in God.

As most of us do when something bad happens to us, Agnes asked why these terrible things happened to her and to her family. She held God responsible for it. She thought of God as an all-powerful being who stood outside the world. For her God was like a man who sees a little girl drowning, could save her if he wanted to, but deliberately refuses to help. Any decent human being would do what they could. But God, who is totally powerful, does nothing.

So Agnes asked why God would act so brutally. She went back to her childhood image of God as a judge who rewards good people and punishes bad people. So she had to believe that her family had sinned terribly if God allowed them to suffer so greatly. But Agnes revolted against this idea. She knew that her daughter and mother were good people. She rejected the kind of a God who causes people to suffer.

Agnes had once found in God the answer to the large questions of her life. She found a way to live in obeying God's law. Her God was one who was over the world as a judge, and arranged events in such a way that rewarded the good and punished the evil. When she faced suffering she could not accept this kind of God. God was a problem, and not an answer to the deep questions she asked. She looked elsewhere to find the meaning of her life and a way to live in the world.

It would not have helped Agnes if someone had given her reasons why God acted justly in letting her suffer. She did not want reasons but a better and 'truer' God. Her kind of God was believable as long as things went well. He could be part of the meaning of a superficial life. But a God who could help her find meaning in the terrible turn her life had taken would need to be much deeper, much more involved.

Agnes did not find this kind of God. And we can only feel with her in her loss of both family and faith. Other Christians have found this God in Jesus. They are able to say that they have found in Jesus Christ the Son of God who shares our human experience, and particularly our suffering. This understanding of God helps them to live with faith during the dark times. But why do we say that Jesus is the Son of God, and how does this help us grapple with life's hard questions?

Jesus as the Son of God

For the early Christians Jesus was the answer to all life's large questions. They saw God in Jesus and recognised what kind of a God he was. The kind of God we know in Jesus is a God who loves us enough to share our weaknesses, invites rather than forces us, and comes to us through weakness and not strength. God and Jesus are welded together. If we want to know what God is like, we look at Jesus.

The early Christians recognised this instinctively. They prayed to God through Jesus. They recognised that all that God gave them came through Jesus. They could not think of Jesus without also thinking of God. Nor could they think of God without thinking of Jesus. For them Jesus was the face of God. So they spoke of Jesus as the Son of God.

When they described Jesus as the Son of God they remembered that Jesus lived a real human life like theirs. Through his daily life, Jesus helped them to see what God was like. Jesus was tempted, perplexed and afraid, and called on God for help. Like us, he called God 'Father'. To call Jesus God's son also revealed that the centre of Jesus' life was his relationship to the Father to whom he prayed.

John's Gospel, which presents Jesus as a mysterious and solemn person, makes it clear that our way to God is through Jesus' life. Jesus says, 'He who has seen me has seen the Father.'

Later Christians reflected deeply on Jesus' relationship to God. They asked what this intimate relationship meant. They saw it, as Paul had also seen it, as the journey of the Son of God into a far country, which involved an exchange between God and humanity. The Son of God came to live a human life, sharing in the messiness of our world, so that we might share in his divinity. The Son of God accepted a human death in order to share God's life with us through his resurrection.

This journey of Jesus as the Son of God and the exchange between God and humanity are beautifully expressed in many Christmas carols. The maker of the stars was the baby to whom wise men were guided by a star. They brought gifts to the one who gave us the whole world as his gift. Behind these lovely images is the conviction that God himself came into our world in Jesus, and that as the Son of God Jesus was all that the Father was – one in being with the Father, as the Nicene Creed says. God does not send an employee to rescue us. God sends family.

If we see Jesus as the Son of God who lived a fully human life like ours, we cannot imagine God as distant, looking at our suffering without caring about it. In his preaching the Son of God depended on human beings and on our response. When he was rejected, he went to his death. Through his suffering he freed us from our murderousness. So God grieves for us in our suffering, because in Jesus he has shared it. And he waits to share with us the full and rich life of Jesus' rising.

The understanding that Jesus is the Son of God who took on our humanity can sound complicated. But many Christians have found the reality very simple. When they are ill and in pain, they have found the image of Jesus on the cross very powerful. It reminds them that Jesus still hangs there like them and with them. God is sharing in their suffering.

In this kind of God we find meaning in the hardest places of our lives. We also find ourselves drawn to follow Jesus in sharing other people's sufferings compassionately. Compassion is a gift of the Holy Spirit whom Jesus promised to give us. Why the Holy Spirit strengthens the faith of some but leaves others, like Agnes, desolate, is a great mystery. It leads us to prayer.

> When Martha heard that Jesus was coming, she went and met him, while Mary stayed at home. Martha said to Jesus, 'Lord, if you had been here, my brother would not have died. But even now I know that God will give you whatever you ask of him.' Jesus said to her, 'Your brother will rise again.' Martha said to him, 'I know that he will rise again in the resurrection on the last day.' Jesus said to her, 'I am the resurrection and the life. Those who believe in me, even though they die, will live, and everyone who lives and believes in me will never die. Do you believe this?' She said to him, 'Yes, Lord, I believe that you are the Messiah, the Son of God, the one coming into the world.'
>
> John 11:20–27

The symbol of the cross

Although Jesus' death on the cross was central in Christian faith, Christians did not originally represent it in art. Crucifixion was a terrifying and shameful form of execution. To paint it would be like painting a man dying in the electric chair.

The centre of the universe

The symbol of the cross quietly became part of Christian life. Critics of Christianity even accused Christians of worshipping it. Christian writers noted that it represented North, South, East and West, and so the whole universe. They saw Christ's cross as being at the centre of the created world.

The sign of God's power

People made the sign of the cross as a sign of God's power to drive out demons and overcome temptation. Its popularity was increased when, in 312 CE, Emperor Constantine fought a decisive battle under a symbol that looked like a cross. His victory freed Christians from persecution. Constantine's mother was then credited with finding the true cross in Jerusalem. Relics of the cross spread throughout the empire.

The sign of God's solidarity with us

The cross has also been a sign of solidarity with the suffering. It hangs over hospital beds reminding patients that the Son of God is there with them (hangs with them) in their pain. In a home for homeless men, many of them affected by alcoholism, a battered cross hangs in the chapel, and above it the words, 'I thirst'. A roughly drawn cross very popular in Cambodia has one of Christ's legs shorter than the other. It remembers the countless victims of landmines in the nation, and associates them with Christ in his suffering.

The cross is the symbol of Jesus' death. It represents the power of God coming through human weakness. So we can find in the cross God's power to save us, and also God's companionship with us in all our weakness.

Baptism at Balding Bay

Balding Bay is a beautiful beach on Magnetic Island, just off Townsville. The pose of the central figures (Christ and John the Baptist) is taken from Piero della Francesca's *Baptism* painting, circa 1442.

John is wearing a blue wetsuit as he baptises Christ with water pouring from a coconut shell.

Christ is wearing the outfit of a lifesaver (known as lifeguards these days). This is an allusion to the saving power of Christ the Saviour. 'Arcadian' is the name of a Life Saving Club on Magnetic Island. An 'Arcadian' lifestyle conveys the image of a pastoral, rustic, simple and innocent lifestyle; this is an allusion to the humbleness of Christ.

The woman in the water is a reference to Mary Magdalene in a pose taken from Manet's *Dejeuner sur l'herbe* painting.

Containers of vinegar are set up on all swimming beaches in Northern Queensland and used in the emergency treatment of marine stinger (Box Jellyfish) bites. The vinegar is a reference to the vinegar Jesus will be offered on the cross. The red writing and the red lid on the vinegar suggest the red wine of the sacrament of the Eucharist.

The silver gull represents the Holy Spirit. The three trees, an allusion to the Trinity, are Norfolk Island pines. These trees have somewhat horizontal branches and are a reference to the three crosses on Calvary.

There are storm clouds building up on the horizon, symbolising trouble ahead.

9: Jesus and the Church

If you work with young adults you meet many generous and gifted people. They have high ideals, are intelligent, are deeply spiritual and often have a deep faith as well, and want to make a difference in the world they are entering. Some remain people of great potential but never quite find a way of living out their ideals effectively. But for others, something happens and everything comes together. They find a way to live generously and also to be nurtured in their lives.

That happened to two young women I met. Anna and Sarina had good jobs, were brought up as Catholics and went to Catholic schools, had good and generous friends. But they wanted something more. It was not easy to find. But then an opportunity came up, and they took it.

As so often happens, they met a few other young people with similar hopes. These other young people had become involved in Vinnies (St. Vincent de Paul Society), and were trying to encourage still other young people to join them in their work. They invited Anna and Sarina to join them in visiting needy people in their area. Anna and Sarina were moved by what they saw and continued to be involved. As they became friends with the people who invited them into this work, their Vinnies work became more and more important in their lives, and Anna and Sarina encouraged still other young adults to become involved.

Through their involvement, Anna and Sarina found that the rest of their lives became richer and more interconnected. They found that faith and prayer became real. The demanding encounters of their work invited them to pray for the people they met and for themselves. They found that the stories of Jesus in the Gospel came alive through their Vinnies work. They also found new and attractive aspects of the Church in their meetings and conversations with their other young friends.

They found that their gifts were complementary. Anna was a good strategic thinker. She could see needs and possibilities, and imagine ways of meeting them. Sarina had enormous energy and confidence in talking with people. She could turn Anna's plans into reality. The benefit for the people whom Vinnies serve was huge. It was also great for Sarina and Anna.

What struck me about Anna and Sarina's story was how it was not simply their own story. It was all about connecting with people. They met a group of young people and connected with them and their work, and then connected with the poor people whom they accompanied. Through being with the poor they found something that enriched them. Conversations with these poor people enabled Anna and Sarina to deepen their faith and to connect with even more people. It made the Church more real for them, and gave them a framework for understanding the stories of Jesus in the Gospel and the ways in which Jesus continues to be present in our world today.

When we ask the large questions of our lives, we so often find the answers only when we are in conversation with others. What they say and, even more importantly, the parts of their lives they invite us into lead us to see the world from another place. We can then enter more deeply into the answers that we have already been given to these large questions.

If Jesus is the answer to our deep questions, we will find him in community with others who, with us, form the body of Christ.

Finding Jesus

Where do we find Jesus and hold him as the answer to the large questions we ask? The Gospel suggests that we find Jesus within a group of disciples. Luke tells the story of two disciples who left Jerusalem after Jesus was killed. They believed that it was all over, that their hopes in him had come to nothing. Then they met a stranger on the road who explained that Jesus' death was part of God's plan. They invited him to dinner, and recognised that he was Jesus as they broke bread together. They then went straight back to Jerusalem to gather with the other disciples. That was where Jesus had led them, and where they could find him and spread the word about him to others.

The gospels too are the books of the communities of disciples. The writers were not neutral historians but were followers of Jesus who had seen in Jesus the heart of God's answer to their deepest questions. They wrote to strengthen the faith of their fellow Christians in their communities by helping them to see the meaning of Jesus in their own lives and to understand the faith and practices of their little community, the church. The attractive picture of Jesus which we find in the stories of the gospels from each community was written to encourage faith in Christ within that community. For them it would not have made any sense to separate Jesus from the Christian community.

St Paul caught the connection between the Church and Jesus by calling the Church the body of Christ, and speaking of the place of the Spirit. The Holy Spirit makes Christ present in the Church and makes him come alive as we read the scriptures and share the Eucharistic meal. (Christ reveals and offers himself in the bread and wine of the Eucharist.) The Spirit also gathers us together around Christ, so that we become Christ's body. By the work of the Spirit both the Christian community and the Eucharist are the body of Christ.

It is through the power of the Holy Spirit that we find the answers to our big questions in Jesus, and that we find the energy and enthusiasm to follow his way. So, it is natural to find Jesus in the community of the Church and to find encouragement from other Christians in living our lives generously.

This is a very ordinary process, as all significant things are in human life. Our hearts are touched through our hands and our feet. The ordinary places of meeting Jesus are through the sacraments. There we hear God's word and Jesus' story together, are usually offered a chance to reflect on what Jesus might mean for our own lives, and meet Jesus as the one who feeds us, who is our companion in marriage, our deepest relationship, and is the one who heals us, forgives us and so on. The sacraments are the ordinary, everyday points of our lives where we are brought again into contact with Jesus.

> All who believed were together and had all things in common; they would sell their possessions and goods and distribute the proceeds to all, as any had need. Day by day, as they spent much time together in the temple, they broke bread at home and ate their food with glad and generous hearts, praising God and having the goodwill of all the people. And day by day the Lord added to their number those who were being saved.
> Acts 2:44–47

But the Church is also the place where we can dream large dreams that take us out of our everyday lives into demanding commitments. It is the place where our imagination can be touched by the story of Jesus and by the desire to live bigger lives, which enable us to love more generously in our own lives. These large desires and big movements of our heart are God's grace and gift. But we need to be open to the Spirit to discern God's grace and gifts.

When we are moved by Jesus' words and actions in the gospel stories, we find the Church to be a place where we can find companions who are touched in the same way and want to share in doing something that will make a difference. At World Youth Day many young people were most moved by finding so many other young people for whom Jesus was at the heart of their lives. They had thought themselves alone but found that they had many companions. This kind of companionship through the centuries has been the start of great things. It carries on God's wish that all should find the meaning of their lives in the generous love that he shows us in making us and in sharing his life with us through Jesus.

Growth of the Church

The early growth of the church is described in the Acts of the Apostles. It included many significant steps.

The sending of the Spirit
The first step was the sending of the Spirit at the time of Jesus' resurrection. The disciples gathered after Jesus appeared to them. When their faith came alive with the sending of the Spirit, they went out and spoke boldly of Jesus as the heart of what matters.

Moving among non-Jewish people
The second step was the decision to accept non-Jewish people into the Church without imposing on them the duty to be circumcised and to follow in detail the Law of Moses. This meant that the Church extended beyond the group of Jews who believed in Christ. Paul was free to preach to people from other religious and cultural backgrounds.

Moving into Europe
The third large symbolic step was the spread of the Gospel into Europe. Rome was the centre of the empire, and Paul's going there as a prisoner showed that faith in Christ was for the whole world and all cultures. It did not belong simply to Palestine and her emigrant communities.

Life in the early Church
The Acts of the Apostles describes the early Church in glowing terms. Those who believed in Christ held their property in common, gave to each according to their need, gathered to pray every day, celebrated the Eucharist together, and quickly attracted others to join them in their faith. This picture has inspired Christian communities ever since.

Paul's letters offer us a realistic story of day-to-day life in the early Church. It was very like the churches of our own day. There was great generosity. There were also failures to live the Gospel, quarrels over issues that were central to being Christ's Church, selfish behaviour, struggles over leadership, and genuine struggles to find Christ's will for the Church.

But one thing remained constant. The early Christians were convinced that in following Christ in their communities they found what mattered most to them.

Reading Jesus

25 EVENTS FROM THE LIFE OF JESUS AND WHERE TO FIND THEM IN THE GOSPELS

Event	Matthew	Mark	Luke	John
Annunciation			1:26-38	
Visitation			1:39-56	
Birth of Jesus	1:18-25		2:1-7	
Adoration of the shepherds			2:8-20	
The wise men and the star of Bethlehem	2:1-12			
Presentation of Jesus in the temple			2:21-38	
Flight into Egypt	2:13-15			
Finding Jesus in the temple			2:41-51	
Ministry of John the Baptist	3:1-12	1:1-8	3:1-20	1:6-8, 19-34
Baptism of Jesus	3:13-17	1:9-11	3:21-22	
Temptation of Jesus	4:1-11	1:12-13	4:1-13	
First disciples of Jesus	4:18-22	1:16-20, 2:13-14 (Matthew)	5:1-11	1:35-51
Beatitudes	5:3-12		6:20-23	
Commissioning the twelve apostles	10:1-14	3:13-19	6:12-16	
Transfiguration of Jesus	17:1-13	9:2-13	9:28-36	
Bread of life discourse				6:22-59
Palm Sunday	21:1-11	11:1-11	19:29-44	12:12-19
Last Supper	26:20-29	14:18-25	22:14-20	13:1-31
Arrest and trial of Jesus	26:47-27:26	14:43-15:15	22:47-23:25	18:1-19:16
Crucifixion of Jesus	27:27-61	15:16-47	23:26-54	19:17-38
Resurrection of Jesus	28:2-10	16:2-8	24:1-12	20:1-18
Road to Emmaus appearance			24:13-32	
Great commission	28:16-20	16:14-18	24:44-49	20:21-23
Jesus appears to Thomas				20:24-29
Ascension of Jesus			24:50-53	

Jesus Prays

Jesus prays many times in the Gospels, in different situations and for different reasons.
He prayed before critical events in his life. He prayed alone and with and for others.
He taught others how to pray. Here is a list of some of the occasions when Jesus prays.

Description	Matthew	Mark	Luke	John
At his baptism			3:21-22	
Before choosing his apostles			6:12-13	
The 'Lord's Prayer'	6:9-15		11:1-4	
Transfiguration			9:28-29	
To give thanks and praise	11:25-26		10:21	
Jesus prays alone	14:23	1:35, 6:46	5:16, 6:12, 9:18	

Before miracles:
    Feeding 5000
    Feeding 4000
    Healing a deaf man
    Raising Lazarus to life
	14:19
	15:36
		6:41
		8:6-7
		7:31-35
			9:16	6:11
				
				11:41-42

Parables on prayer:
    The persistent friend
    The unjust judge
    The Pharisee and the tax collector
			11:5-13
			18:1-8
			18:9-14	

Praying for others	19:13		22:31-32	17:1-26
Last Supper	26:26-28	14:22-24	22:17-20	
In the garden of Gethsemane	26:36-45	14:32-41	22:39-46	

On the cross:
    Father, forgive them
    My God, my God, why have you forsaken me?
    Into your hands I commend my spirit
	
	27:46
		
		15:34
			23:34
			
			23:46	

Asking for help				12:27-28

Teaching on prayer:
    Pray for those who persecute you
    Go to your room and shut the door
    Forgive others
    Ask, seek, knock
    If two or three of you agree about anything you ask, it will be done for you
    Whatever you ask for in prayer with faith you will receive
 	
    Be alert at all times, praying
	5:44
	6:5-8
	6:14-15
	7:7-11
	18:19-20
	
	21:22
		
		11:25
		
		11:24
			6:27-28
			
			11:9-13
			
			21:36
				
				14:13-16
				15:7
				16:23-24

Lord, teach us to pray

JESUS SAID, PRAY THEN IN THIS WAY:

Our Father in heaven,
hallowed be your name.
Your kingdom come.
Your will be done,
on earth as it is in heaven.
Give us this day our daily bread.
And forgive us our debts,
as we also have forgiven our debtors.
And do not bring us to
the time of trial,
but rescue us from the evil one.

MATTHEW 6:9-13
(ALSO LUKE 11:1-4)

www.ingramcontent.com/pod-product-compliance
Lightning Source LLC
Chambersburg PA
CBHW061059170426
43199CB00025B/2940